ISBN 978-1-5285-2732-3
PIBN 10896981

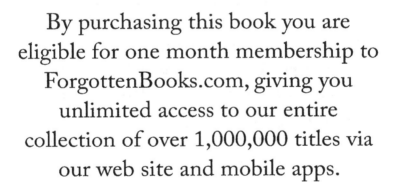

English
Français
Deutsche
Italiano
Español
Português

www.forgottenbooks.com

Mythology Photography **Fiction**
Fishing Christianity **Art** Cooking
Essays Buddhism Freemasonry
Medicine **Biology** Music **Ancient**
Egypt Evolution Carpentry Physics
Dance Geology **Mathematics** Fitness
Shakespeare **Folklore** Yoga Marketing
Confidence Immortality Biographies
Poetry **Psychology** Witchcraft
Electronics Chemistry History **Law**
Accounting **Philosophy** Anthropology
Alchemy Drama Quantum Mechanics
Atheism Sexual Health **Ancient History**
Entrepreneurship Languages Sport
Paleontology Needlework Islam
Metaphysics Investment Archaeology
Parenting Statistics Criminology
Motivational

CONTENTS

****

September 28th, 1918

The Director,
    National Park Service,
        Washington, D. C.

Sir:

Reference to my annual report dated September 25, enclosed herewith, corrections and additions will be transmitted at an early date as follows:

Statement of travel, pages 7 to 9 will later be brought down to date.

Page 15, report of G. Clyde Baldwin not yet received; will be transmitted soon as received.

Page 30, report of Mr. W. T. Thompson, Supt. Fisheries Statoio, not yet received. Will be transmitted soon as received.

I hope a little later to have a few interesting photographs to illustrate some of the main features of the enclosed report, and will transmit them.

                    Very respectfully,
                    (signed) Chester A. Lindsley
                        Acting Superintendent.

Inclosure.

The Director,
        National Park Service,
            Washington, D. C.

Sir:

In compliance with your request of August 23, 1918, I
have the honor to submit annual report of condition of affairs
in, and the management of, Yellowstone National Park during
the past fiscal year.

The Yellowstone National Park was set aside by act of
Congress approved March1, 1872 (secs. 2474 and 2475, R. S.;
17 Stat., 32), as a pleasure ground for the benefit and en-
joyment of the people and placed under the control of the
Secretary of the Interior. It is situated principally in
northwestern Wyoming but laps over a little more than two
miles into Montana on the north and almost two miles into
Montene and Idaho on the west. Its dimensions are about 62
miles north and south and about 54 miles east and west, giving
an area of about 3,348 square miles, or 2,142,720 acres. Its
altitude is 6,000 to 11,000 feet.

During the first fourteen years of its existence as a
National Park, the Yellowstone was administered by civilian
superintendents, appointed by the Secretary of the Interior,
assisted, when funds were available for salaries, by a few
civilian scouts. At that time the country was new and wild,
and filled with lawless characters of all sorts. This method

of governing the park was sometimes unsatisfactory for the reason
that funds were insufficient to employ enough scouts to properly
police the vast area to be protected, and I understand that in
some instances the employees were selected for political reasons
without reference to their adaptability for the duties required.
By Act of Congress approved March 3, 1883, the Secretary of the
Interior **was authorized to call upon the Secretary of War** to
make the necessary details of troops to guard the park, but **it**
was not until August 20, 1886, that the civilian force was
finally relieved by officers and enlisted men of the United
States Army as guardians of the park, the Commanding Officer of
troops serving also in the capacity of Acting Superintendent of the
park under the direct supervision of the Secretary of the Interior.
Many most efficient and able officers of the Army have held the
responsible position at the head of the administration and protection of Yellowstone Park, and records wore established of which
they may well be proud. But conditions have changed, and the
National Parks have grown in number and popularity to such an
extent as to warrant the establishment by Congress of a regular
Bureau in Washington for their administration and management under
modern business methods, and this Bureau has been recognized as
the natural and proper medium through which all park activities
are to be prosecuted, by the Act of Congress approved July 1,
1918, (Sundry Civil Bill) which provides the total sum of

$334,920.00 for administration, protection, maintenance, and
improvement in Yellowstone National Park. Under this Act the
Corps of Engineers of the Army was, on July 1st, relieved of
the duties of building and maintaining roads, bridges and other
improvements. The responsibility of the protection of the park
has been taken over from the commanding officer of troops, the
stations in the park have been garrisoned by civilian rangers,
and orders are expected daily for the permanent abandonment of
Fort Yellowstone, releasing the troops which are needed by the
War Department for important work elsewhere.

Park Headquarters are located at Mammoth Hot Springs, 5
miles from the northern entrance. Fifteen Ranger Stations are
maintained at convenient points throughout the park, and these
are connected with Headquarters by 270 miles of telephone lines.
There are 278.8 miles of main road and 24.75 miles of secondary
road to maintain inside of the park, and 106.5 miles of main
road to maintain in the forest reserves adjoining the park on
the south and east. Nearly 400 miles of fairly well marked
trails are also available for use of those desiring to travel
on horseback.

TRAVEL

Before the opening of the tourist season, much doubt ex-
isted as to the probable effect of the war conditions on tourist
travel to the National Parks, and many, more especially the
concessionors, were very pessimistic as to the prospects. In

March it was officially announced through the press that the Yellowstone Park tourist season would extend from June 25 to September 15. From March until the season finally opened, many rumors were current to the effect that the park would not open due to war conditions, and these had to be contradicted many times. It was not until June 17th that I was notified by wire that the hotels would not open, and this information going out through the press and by various other methods was often interpreted to mean that the park was closed, and doubtless resulted in travel being discouraged to a considerable extent. The lateness of this announcement resulted to some extent in hardship to other concessioners, but the Camping Company profited by the change, as it left to them all travel except those providing their own camping facilities, instead of dividing it with the hotels. This enabled the Camping Company to make a fair showing and operate at a reasonable profit, whereas if the hotels had also been opened, both would have operated at a loss.

The latter part of May and early in June the weather was much warmer than usual, and in June 2.97 inches of rainfall was recorded, which was about one-third more than the normal for June. These conditions, taken together, resulted in extremely high water, with an increase amount of damage to roads from washouts. The railroad on the Park Branch to Livingston was washed out in several places so we had no train into Gardiner from

June 12th to June 21st, inclusive, and it was not until June 19th
that arrangements were finally made to bring the mail from
Livingston by automobile. The road through Gardiner Canyon was
washed out so as to be impassable after June 10th, and the old
road over the hill back of Mammoth Hotel, which was repaired
at an expense of about $4,000, has been in use ever since. This
was no special disappointment, however, as we had expected the
Gardiner Slide to close the canyon road permanently, and the old
road had been put in condition for travel with this in view. The
old road is longer, narrow, and very slippery after heavy rains,
but it is considered only for temporary use until the Gardiner
Canyon road can be restored, and an appropriation of $50,000 is
now available for that purpose. One-way schedules were necessary on
it about train time, when travel was heaviest, and while no serious
accidents occurred, much inconvenience was caused by meeting of
vehicles on this road.

The roads to Norris and the west side of the park were open
at the end of May.

On the day of opening for tourist travel, the roads on the
regular park tour were open for travel except from the eastern
entrance to the belt line, and between Canyon and Tower Falls
through Dunraven Pass. The regular travel was routed through Dunraven Pass beginning July 8th, but on a few occasions during the
season, when heavy storms have occurred, it was not considered

safe, and the regular cars came in via Norris. The road between
the eastern entrance and Cody was very badly damaged by the Juno
floods, and for a time the chances for travel from that direction
looked slim. But the citizens of Cody did much temporary repair
work at their own expense, and succeeded in getting a special appropriation of $25,000 additional to the regular appropriation,
for repairing the unusual damage between the Lake Hotel and Cody.
A few private automobiles came in from the Cody entrance on July
2d, but they had to be dragged across two huge snowbanks in Sylvan
Pass with ropes, and it was not until July 13th that the road was
considered safe for regular travel, and the Yellowstone Park Transportation Company established its regular daily schedule to trains
at Cody.

The bridge across Lamar River, on the road between Tower
Fells and Cooke City, was washed away on June 11th, and from then
until August 8th travel to Cooke was relayed from Lamar River,
which was crossed in a small car hung on a wire cable.

The Transportation Company maintained a regular twice-a-week
service to Jackson Hole, beginning July 15th, but it was not
patronized to any great extent.

The aggregate number of persons visiting the park during the
year ended September 30, 1918 was as follows:

Yellowstone Park Transportation Company:

```
Entering via the northern entrance.......1557
Entering via the western entrance........1136
Entering via the eastern entrance........ 333   3026
```

Making park trips with private transportation:

```
    With automobiles, paid and compli-
      mentary.................................16530
    With automobiles, second trip............  698
                                              17228
    Wlth motorcycles.........................   25
    With bicycles............................    3
    With other transportation as "private
      camping parties".......................  474  17730
    Miscellaneous short trips.....................   430

              Grand total....................  21196
```

8.   As a matter of economy, the National Park Service required

the Camping Company to open but three of its permanent camps,

namely, Mammoth, Geysers, (at Upper Basin) and Canyon, thus

saving the expense of running the Lake Camp, the camp at Lost

Creek, near Tower Falls, and the lunch station near the western

entrance.   This arrangement required a much less overhead ex-

pense, and gave better assurance of a paying business at the be-

ginning of a very doubtful season, and caused but very little, if

any, dissatisfaction on the part of the tourists.   Instead of

staying one night at Lake Camp, the distance from Upper Basin to

Canyon was covered in one afternoon's drive, leaving an extra

day for viewing the more interesting wonders at Upper Basin and

Canyon.   The Camping Company reports that 68,257 meals and 26,407

lodgings were served at the camps during the season:

TRAVEL BY DIFFERENT ENTRANCES

```
From the north, via Gardiner, Montana...................7499
From the west, via Yellowstone, Montana.................8685
From the east, via Cody, Wyoming.......................4399
From the south, via Jackson, Wyoming...................  537
From the northeast, via Cooke, Montana.................   66
                                            .............21186
```

PRIVATE AUTOMOBILE TRAVEL

	Autos.	Tourists.
Entering via the northern entrance	1511	5363
Entering via the western entrance	1938	7341
Entering via the eastern entrance	1127	3992
Entering via the southern entrance	134	532
Total	4710	17228

A fee of $7.50 was charged for automobile tickets of passage and $2.50 for motorcycle tickets of passage, which were good for the entire season. Complimentary tickets were issued to officials of adjoining States or counties, and to officials of the Federal Government, visiting the park officially.

AUTOMOBILE TRAVEL BY STATES

A statement showing the automobile travel, by states, in Yellowstone National Park, for the season of 1918 follows:

Private Travel in Yellowstone National Park, by States.

	North Entrance	West Entrance	East Entrance	South Entrance	Totals
Alabama		3			3
Arkansas		12	22		34
Arizona	2	30	14	4	50
California	95	266	84	11	456
Colorado	66	137	291	9	502
Connecticut	2	2	6		10
Dist. of Columbia			14	2	16
Delaware	3				3
Florida		3	30		33
Idaho	60	2350	26	256	2692
Illinois	64	41	47		152
Indiana	31	20	10		61
Iowa	119	50	56	2	235
Kansas	44	107	141	8	300
Kentucky	2				2
Louisiana		6	5		11
Massachusetts	5	2			7
Michigan	29	22	50		101
Minnesota	186	17	21		224
Mississippi	2	3	12		17
Missouri	26	56	122	2	206
Montana	3071	1605	390	4	5070
Nebraska	78	95	356		529
Nevada	5	54	9		68
New Jersey	3	4	10		17
New Mexico		10	29		39
New York	24	21	14	2	61
North Dakota	276	34	31		341
Ohio	31	25	34		90
Oklahoma	14	58	170		242
Oregon	109	158	21		288
Pennsylvania	17	6	14		37
Rhode Island	2				2
South Dakota	111	10	91	4	216
Tennessee		3	8		11
Texas	18	54	91		163
Utah	68	1637	35	114	1854
Virginia	3				3
Washington	399	197	52		648
West Virginia		4			4
Wisconsin	103	27	13		143
Wyoming	180	147	1668	95	2
Canada	50	10	3	6	69
Total	5208	72 4	3000		

All but a very small percentage of tourists visiting the
park traveled by motor transportation. The total travel, as com-
pared with the past three years, was small. But it was better than
many anticipated at the beginning of the season, although the number coming to the park by rail was relatively small, due to the
fact that the railroads rather discouraged travel for pleasure during
the busy war times.

Camping shelters, wood and toilet facilities, were furnished
free to parties touring with their own cars and camping out. While
we did not always have sufficient labor available to give these
camps proper attention, they were appreciated and complaints were
few.

No movable-camp licenses were issued for wagon and saddle
horse transportation.

Special permits were issued to parties holding properties in
the mining camp of Cooke, Montana, to use their motors for hauling
supplies to and from Gardiner, Montana, through the park as follows:

Nels E. Soderholm.
Yellowstone Mining Corporation.
Western Smelting & Power Company.
Buffalo-Montana Company

These parties have done comparatively little hauling, and
what they have done has been rather expensive for them, due to
the fact that they expended considerable money repairing the road
and bridges after the high water had washed them out in many
places.

Motor cars and trucks were generally used by different branches of the Government, and by concessioners, in handling regular business in the park. Special permits for these were issued without charge.

CONCESSIONS

All concessioners operating in the park showed their usual fine spirit of co-operation, and complaints from the public resulting from any friction between different interests were practically unknown during the summer.

As in every line of work, due to unusual war conditions, all kinds of labor and supplies are scarce, and economy under all conditions is a virtue. Consequently additions to plant, improvement of buildings, and similar work that can be postponed, is discouraged, and only actual necessary expenditures for maintenance is encouraged. For those reasons, many improvements under consideration by concessioners were not made.

The Yellowstone Park Hotel Company did not open any of its hotels in the park, and only a keeper for each hotel was employed.

The only accommodations available in the park were at the Mammoth, Upper Basin, and Canyon Camps, operated by the Yellowstone Park Camping Company. The fact that the hotels did not open, made business fairly good for the Camping Company, even though travel was light. As a rule the accommodations were excellent, and complaints were few. A new building was constructed at Mammoth Camp,

satisfactory from an architectural standpoint, it serves its purpose well and added much to the comfort and pleasure of the public. A garage for taking care of private automobiles was also built at Mammoth. At Upper Basin Camp but little improvement work was done, due to scarcity of labor. A new laundry was constructed. An extension to the log dining room, commenced late last fall, is still unfinished, though it was badly needed during the height of the season. At Grand Canyon Camp a rough log building was erected for use as a laundry, and a large warehouse and a garage are under construction.

The Yellowstone Park Transportation Company operated the only transportation line in the park, and handled all travel from the trains at Gardiner, Yellowstone, and Cody. As this kind of travel was light, only a small part of the extensive plant of this company was in use during the season. The service was improved over the 1917 season; drivers were usually careful, and attentive to passengers, and complaints were few. A new garage, 50 x 200 feet in size, was built by this company close to the Lake Hotel late last fall, but has not been put in use as there was no stopping place at the Lake during the season.

Practically no business was done by the Yellowstone Park Boat Company during the summer, as there was no opportunity to patronize the boats, due to the lack of accommodations for the night at the Lake Outlet. A few of the motor and other boats were inspected by

a representative of the Steamboat Inspection Service, for use in case there was any demand for them. The Boat Company's store at Lake Outlet was run by Mr. C. A. Hamilton, as a branch of his main store at Upper Geyser Basin.

n   Mr. George Whittaker had his post office store at Mammoth Hot Springs open throughout the year. He also ran a general store at Grand Canyon, during the tourist season, his contract with the National Park Service having been extended for a term of years to cover this additional business. The Hotel Company's extensive vegetable garden, located at the head of Gardiner Canyon, and which was planted as usual last spring for use of hotels, was taken over by Mr. Whittaker when it was decided not to open the hotels, and the crops have been marketed by him, mostly to our road construction camps, at cost. This was done at a loss to the Hotel Company, and with but little, if any, profit to Mr. Whittaker, at my request as food conservation measure.

Mr. C. A. Hamilton did a fairly good business at his general store at Upper Basin, and also ran the Lake Store, as heretofore noted.

Mr. J. E. Haynes kept his shops at Mammoth and Upper Basin open throughout the season, as well as maintaining booths in the three permanent camps. He also kept the picture shop and inform- ation bureau at Tower Falls open during the most of the summer. A small frame building, formerly belonging to the Yellowstone-

Western Stage Company at Mammoth, was, with permission of the National Park Service, moved to the rear of his residence and studio, for use as a storehouse.

The bath house at Upper Geyser Basin was operated under the concession to Frances F. Brothers throughout the season. A total of 2290 persons used these baths, of whom 2029 were tourists and 26 were park employees.

Business was fairly good at the ice cream parlors and curio shop operated by the owners, Mesdames Pryor and Trischman, and this store was kept open throughout the season.

The permit issued during the season of 1917 to Jay Wilcox and Jim Parker, of Gardiner, Montana, to cultivate an acre of ground in Turkey Pen Pass, on Yellowstone River about two miles above Gardiner, was renewed and extended to cover about four acres of land.

Mr. Robert I. McKay, who holds a permit authorizing him to construct a metal-surfaced road through the park between Gardiner and Cooke, Montana, so as to permit of the development and marketing of valuable mineral resources in Cooke, made no progress except to do some surveying for his right-of-way.

STATEMENT OF REVENUE RECEIVED

Revenues were collected from concessioners, sale of automobile and motorcycle tickets, etc., as follows:

Sale of automobile permits................... 39,880.80
Collections from concessioners............... 26,057.81
Camping Party Licenses....................... 172.00
Sale of electric current..................... 1,226.61
Sale of water................................ 176.89
Miscellaneous collections.................... 784.35

Total.................... $ 68,292.46

STREAM GAGING

The following memorandum of work done in the park under this

head is furnished by Mr. C. Clyde Baldwin, District Engineer of

the Water-resources branch of the U. S. Geological Survey, Boise,

Idaho, under whose direction it is carried on:

SUMMARY OF HYDROMETRIC WORK, OCTOBER 1, 1917, TO SEPTEMBER 30, 1918.

Records were obtained at the following gaging-stations which
were established in 1913:

Madison River, near Yellowstone, Montana; Yellowstone River,
above upper falls, in Yellowstone Park; Snake River, at South Boundary of Yellowstone National Park.

Because of frequent changes in the personnel on duty at the
different soldier stations and because of periods when some of the
stations were unoccupied, the gage height records are perhaps less
satisfactory than in former years, but still suffice to afford records at each station except the one on the Yellowstone, throughout
the greater part of the year. The latter was temporarily discontinued during the winter months.

Two series of actual current meter measurements were obtained
at these stations during the year by Survey engineers. During the
month of June a reconnaissance was also made of Tower Creek in the
vicinity of Tower Falls. Because of the high stage of the stream
at that time and the fact that no camp was to be maintained in the
vicinity during the season of 1918 it was not deemed advisable to
install a new station.

A recording gage and the necessary materials for its install-
ation at the Madison River station were purchased during the year

and the actual construction work will be done during the present month (October).

Signs for the guidance of tourists were purchased and installed during the year at each of the three above-mentioned gaging-stations.

Acknowledgments should be made for transportation and subsistence which was furnished free to Survey engineers as during July 1917 by the transportation and camping companies, during the regular park season.

Detailed descriptions of the gaging-stations together with summaries of current meter measurements and discharge data for each will be published in the annual Water-Supply Papers of the United States Geological Survey, Parts IV and VII, respectively, for Missouri and Snake River drainage areas.

While such co-operation as was possible was given Mr. Baldwin by scouts employed by this office, and by soldiers at stations under the Commanding Officer at Fort Yellowstone, changes at the gaging stations have necessarily been so frequent that the work has been rather unsatisfactory during the past year; instructions have been given to rangers recently taking over these stations to give due attention to the rendering of these reports, and of those to the U. S. Weather Bureau, which are also of interest and value.

WEATHER REPORT

A branch office of the U. S. Weather Bureau is maintained at Mammoth Hot Springs in the park, in charge of Mr. G. L. Lawton, Observer, and under his direction and by the use of instruments furnished by his office, temperature and precipitation records are made at 6 of our park stations. These records are of much interest

and practical value.

ROADS AND IMPROVEMENTS

During the early history of the park, and up to the end of
June, 1894, the construction of roads, bridges, etc., in the park
was accomplished by special appropriations under the Secretary of
War, administered by officers of the U. S. Engineer Department.
From July 1, 1894, to June 30, 1899, this appropriations act was
worded so as to permit its expenditure under the Secretary of the
Interior, through the park superintendent, when it was again
changed back and placed under charge of the Engineer Department
of the Army. This was again reversed, by the Sundry Civil Bill
approved July, 1, 1918, which placed all activities in Yellowstone
Park under the jurisdiction of the Secretary of the Interior and
the National Park Service. Therefore, for the period to the end of
June, 1918, this work was done under the direction of the Chief of
Engineers, represented here since November1, 1917, by Major George
B. Verrill, E. O.R.C. Major Verrill has been relieved and gone to
another station, therefore the following notes on the work accomplished under his direction have been taken as best they might,
from his reports:

General road construction and maintenance was continued as
late in the fall of 1917 as the weather permitted. Warm weather
in the spring of 1918 melted the snow rapidly so that small crews
were put on general repair work during May and as much work done

as funds on hand permitted.

In general the work accomplished was as follows:

NORTH APPROACH:

The Gardiner Slide, which for several years has been giving increasing trouble, threatened to entirely close the north approach road. Throughout the summer of 1917 the road was kept open by a small crew, and at the end of October the steam-shovel was put at work cutting off the toe of the slide and throwing the material into the river. Work was continued until January 16, 1918, when the general condition of the road was considered good. However, as soon as the frozen ground began to thaw, the slide movement became so rapid that it was considered impracticable and too expensive to attempt to keep the road open. To keep a means of communication open, work was begun repairing and realigning the old freight road over the hill. Grades were reduced from a maximum of 20% to 10% and necessary bridges and culverts constructed. As an emergency road a width of 10 feet was adopted and no graveling or other improvements attempted. It was necessary to realign 10,000 feet of road and widen and repair the entire five miles; total amount expended was $4,150.00. Early in June a sudden spell of hot weather, followed by heavy rains, caused an exceptionally high freshet in the Gardiner River, which resulted in the complete destruction of nearly 1 mile of the road through the Gardiner

Canyon, causing the abandonment of this road and necessitating
the entire use of the old freight road as a means of communication
with Gardiner and railroad transportation. Owing to the character
of the material of which this road is composed it is very slippery
and muddy in wet weather, but has served its purpose satisfactorily
by reason of the fact that it was built as a temporary road only until the main road could be repaired.

WEST APPROACH:

Nine and one-half miles of this road from the west boundary
have been finished during the past four years with oil macadam.
Of this the first five miles are in excellent condition, the
oiled surface being 18 feet wide and showing little signs of wear.
On the remaining 4½ miles the surface is only 10 feet wide, and
in many places is raveling and breaking badly, so that the general
condition is hardly considered fair. The remaining 4 miles have
not been surfaced but the road is in good condition.

SOUTH APPROACH: (In the park.)

General repairs were continued as late in the fall of 1917
as the weather permitted, but due to heavy snow no work was done
in the spring of 1918. The general condition of the road is good,
except for the numerous wooden bridges and culverts. These are
comparatively temporary, and should be replaced when practicable.

SOUTH APPROACH: (In the Forest Reserve.)

General maintenance on 25 miles of this road and construction

work on Pilgrim Creek Bridge were continued until late in October.
The 366-foot bridge over Pilgrim Creek was about 95% complete at
this time, and needs only a small fill at the north end and hand
rails.

Unusually high waters endangered all bridges during the month
of June, and only strenuous efforts by rangers saved the bridges
at Pilgrim Creek and Snake River. Small damage was done the approaches to the Pilgrim Creek bridge, but the east end of the north
pier of the Snake River bridges settled about 2 feet, badly twist-
ing the steel truss of 100-foot span, but not seriously damaging
it.

EAST APPROACH: (In the park.)

General repair work was continued until late in October,
when Sylvan Pass was blocked with snow. At this time it is still
closed so that no work can be done. High water during June, 1918,
took several piles out of the bents under the Yellowstone River
bridge, but its use is not impaired. The small bridge near Pelican
Creek was washed out but can be crossed.

EAST APPROACH: (In the Forest Reserve.)

General maintenance work was continued until the end of the
season throughout the 28 miles of road. Exceptionally high waters,
said to be the highest on record, washed the road out in about
22 places, in most cases taking out the entire roadway, undermined
the east abutment of the Pahaska Bridge and the west abutment of the

21

North Fork bridge, as well as taking out the west approach of
the North Fork bridge. As a result, the road is impassable at
this time, but it is understood that the people of Cody and vicinity are at work making temporary by-pass roads.

COOKE CITY ROAD:

The maintenance crew was removed from this road in September,
due to scarcity of labor, and no furhher repair work done until
May, 1918, when a small repair crew was sent over the entire
length. However, the high water in June took out the log bridges
over the Lamar River, about 180 feet long, and Soda Butte and
Pebble Creeks, thus completely closing traffic. This road is used
principally by private interests in Cooke City, so that at this
time traffic is being maintained by a cableway across the Lamar
River and detours, with fords across the smaller creeks.

MAIN BELT LINE:

General repairs and grader work were continued throughout the
season. An early spring allowed flying grader crews to get out in
May. Frequent rains made the roads muddy and easily rutted, and so
far no sprinkling has been necessary.

Work was continued on the Firehole Realignment until October
23, 1917, at which time 5,700 feet had been completed; another 1,000
feet was about 50% complete, and the remaining 1,000 feet had not been
started.

Work on the waterbound macadam base between Norris and Mammoth
Hot Springs was discontinued in September, due to scarcity of labor,

and what men who were left graveled 2,400 feet on the same road
in the vicinity of the Hoodoos. Using dump trucks this road was
graveled an average of 13 feet wide and 5 inches deep. When
rolled this made an excellent road. The cost was at the rate of
$2,000.00 per mile.

An attempt was made during June, 1918, to oil the macadam
base, laid during the season of 1917, and 19,000 gallons of heavy
oil were purchased and stored at Gardiner. Due to wet weather only
one section, 1050 feet long and 14 feet wide, was oiled by the close
of the year.

Bridge and culvert work was done as follows:

1 reinforced concrete culvert 4' x 2'3" x 42' in Dunraven
Pass, 9.2 miles from Canyon Junction.

1 reinforced concrete culvert 4' x 2'3" x 30' Yancey Creek,
1.5 miles west of Tower Falls Station.

1 reinforced concrete culvert 6' x 4' x 72' at Geode Creek,
12½ miles east of Mammoth Hot Springs on Tower Falls road.

1 double reinforced concrete culvert, each opening
6' x 2'3" x 18' on Swan Lake flats, five miles south of
Mammoth Hot Springs.

Same kind of culvert being built at Apollinaris Spring,
10 miles south of Mammoth Hot Springs. (Notcompleted.)

COAL MINE:

Due to the fact that it was seemingly impossible for the
department to purchase a supply of coal for the winter, an old

mine was opened on the face of Mount Everts in October, 1917.
467 tons of coal were mined and delivered to headquarters and
served all purposes. The total cost of the coal, including
development, timbering, and hauling, was $9.27 per ton.

SUNSET PEAK ROAD:

During the spring of 1918 general repairs were made and two
log bridges were built on this road, making it safe for vehicular
traffic.

HEADQUARTERS:

5,500 feet of roads in the vicinity of Mammoth Hot Springs
and Fort Yellowstone were graveled to a width of about 20 feet,
during the spring. After the snow melted general maintenance of
the grounds in the vicinity of Fort Yellowstone and at the northern entrance was continued. Tentative plans for engineer quarters
were prepared and submitted during the winter. Plant and equip-
ment at Headquarters was put in repair so as to be in first-class
condition for the season's work.

PLATFORMS AND BOARD WALKS:

Ten landing platforms at various points of interest, originally
built to accommodate passengers alighting from horse-drawn vehicles,
were lowered to accommodate automobile passengers. In the Norris
Geyser Basin 722 linear feet of new walk was built and 246 linear
feet of old walk repaired. At the Thumb 185 feet of old walk was
repaired, and at Tower Falls a landing platform was built with
steps leading to the top of the bluff.

24

The Sundry Civil Bill, approved July 1, 1918, under National Parks, page 49, reads:

"Yellowstone National Park, Wyoming: For administration, protection, maintenance, and improvement, including not to exceed $7,500 for maintenance of the road in the forest reserve leading out of the park from the east boundary, not to exceed $7,500 for maintenance of the road in the forest reserve leading out of the park from the south boundary, for repairing roads in the park and in adjoining forest reserves from Lake Hotel to the Cody entrance, '2 5,000; not to exceed $7,600 for the purchase, operation, maintenance, and repair of motor-propelled passenger-carrying vehicles, and including feed for buffalo and other animals and salaries of buffalo keepers, $269,520, to be expended by and under the direction of the Secretary of the Interior: Provided, That not exceeding $2,000 may be expended for the removal of snow from any of the roads for the purpose of opening them in advance of the tourist season.

"Hereafter road extensions and improvements shall be made in said park and in harmony with the general plan of roads and improvements to be approved by the Secretary of the Interior.

"For continuing the widening to not exceeding eighteen feet of roadway, improving the surface of roads, and for building bridges and culverts from the belt-line road to the western border, from the Thumb Station to the southern border, and from the Lake Hotel to the eastern border, all within Yellowstone National Park, to

make such roads suitable and safe for animal drawn and motor-propelled vehicles, $15,400.

"For a new road around the Gardiner Slide, $50,000.

"For resurfacing and for finishing the belt line with oil macadam, the unexpended balance of the appropriation for the fiscal year nineteen hundred and eighteen is made available for the fiscal year nineteen hundred and nineteen."

Under the provisions of this bill the improvement and maintenance work has been combined with the work of administration and protection of the park, under this office, the maintenance and improvement work being under the direct charge of Mr. George E. Goodwin, Civil Engineer, National Park Service.

By this combination this Department has undertaken to make a saving of at least $20,000.00, and this I am confident we shall be able to do, in addition to eliminating needless friction and division of authority, and giving much greater efficiency.

At the beginning of the season most of the roads of the park were in the worst condition that they have been for years. The high waters of the last of May and the first of June,- the highest that have been recorded for years, did great damage to most of the roads, and certain sections of roads were entirely washed away and many of the bridges and culverts were either damaged or washed out.

26

The north entrance road, from Gardiner to Mammoth Hot Springs, which was built by General Chittenden in 1900, and which is the most used entrance to the park, was very badly damaged by the floods of the Gardiner River, about three-fourths of a mile of the road through the Gardiner Canyon being entirely washed out, and the bridges were either washed out or the piers undermined and settled out of level. Most of the damaged section of the road had been originally constructed at a large expense, as it was built on a location largely reclaimed, from the original river channel, and consisted of rock and earth fills retained by concrete and stone revetment walls. This section of road was so completely destroyed that a new road will have to be constructed through the canyon on the opposite side of the river, which will involve some very heavy construction, but it will avoid the so-called Gardiner Slide, which has given so much trouble during the past two years and that has at times, for short periods, closed the road to travel.

The eastern entrance, or Cody road, was also badly damaged both within the park and through the National Forest, east of the park, which road is also maintained and improved by this Department. Not less than twelve serious washouts occurred, some of which were several hundred feet in length, and all of which required rock or timber revetment to prevent the Shoshone River from again washing out these pieces of road. Considerable damage was also done to the new steel bridges recently erected as the abutments were badly

undermined and settled and the approaches were washed out.

On the Snake River road, or southern entrance, several small structures were washed out as were the approaches of the Pilgrim Creek bridge and one of the abutments of the new steel bridge across the Snake River was so badly undermined that the bridge was thrown out of transverse level fully two feet, all of which necessitated heavy repairs, both within the park, and in the forest reserve south of the park.

The Belt Line or "Loop Roads" in the park were not so badly damaged as the north, east, and southern entrance roads, but many of the cross drainage structures proved incapable of conveying the floods and were washed out as were many short sections of roads parallelling the streams.

The Corps of Engineers, U. S. Army, made such repairs to the roads as were possible prior to July 1st, and got all of the southern, loop road, the northern and western entrance roads open to travel at the beginning of the park season, either by the construction of temporary roads, as in the case of the northern entrance, or by making the necessary temporary repairs to the damaged roads. The southern and eastern entrance roads were open to travel about the second of July. Most of the first preliminary temporary repairs on the Cody road through the National Forest being made by the people of Cody in order that automobile tourists that had come to the Cody gateway might enter the park as planned.

Great credit is due the public spirited citizens of Cody for their
energetic and timely efforts in this work.

In addition to the ordinary maintenance and repair work of
the roads in the park and the sprinkling of some of the driest and
most dusty stretches, some of the mudiest and heretofore badly
rutted sections of road, were graveled and otherwise improved. Between two and three miles were regraded and graveled between Apollinaris Spring and Norris Basin. Eight steel bridges were also
painted and two small concrete culverts and a number of corrugated
culverts were installed.

The temporary log bridge across the Lamar River, which was
built by the mining interests of Cooke City, to replace the struc-
ture washed out, was strengthened and otherwise improved to accommodate truck hauling, and a crew is at work improving the Cooke
City road.

The extreme shortage of labor made it necessary to confine the work
to the most needed and minor repairs and to delay the heavy recon-
struction work until the park tourist travel had closed for the
season, when it is proposed to repair the Snake River bridge, recon-
struct the Gardiner Canyon road, and complete the repairs of the
Cody road. The general average maintenance and repair force averaged
about 150 men and seventy teams, whereas to have maintained and
completely repaired the roads during the season would have required
at least 350 men and one hundred teams.

29

FISH

The Hatchery, located on the shore of Yellowstone Lake near its outlet, was operated during the summer as usual by the United States Fish Commission, under the direction of Mr. J. T. Thompson, the Superintendent of the Hatchery at Bozeman, Montana. An attempt was made to supplement the work of collecting eggs of the blackspotted trout in the park, by gathering those available at a small lake in Soda Butte Creek, near Soda Butte Station, generally known as Fish Lake. (Not shown on the map.) A man was sent in on June 11th to make this collection, but the same day the Lamar River bridge was washed away, so the eggs could not be brought in without great expense, and the project was abandoned. Mr. Thompson has furnished me with the following notes on his work in the park for the season of 1918:

Fish fry of other varieties were not shipped in for planting in park waters last spring, as usual, on account of the unusual difficulties attending their transportation.

Fishing was excellent throughout the summer, and many fine catches were taken by tourists and employees. No violations of the law were reported. Exception was made as to number to be taken in one day, in favor of the Camping Company, so as to provide the tables at the camps with trout, which are a great treat for tourists.

WILD ANIMALS

The fall of 1917 was beautiful and warm, and winter did not come until late. The road to Sylvan Pass was not opened until

30

October 28; to Snake River until November 9th; and as late as
November 23d the going was good on the west side of the park as
in summer. Even December was 5.6 degrees warmer than normal, so
the game animals were in splendid condition and had plenty of
excellent winter range left for them when the severe weather came
again in March, which was 5.4 degrees warmer than normal, and un-
covered considerable grass on the foothills, making in all a
rather short and favorable winter for elk, deer, antelope, and
mountain sheep, and the loss among them was slight.

The fair weather in October, November and December, was a
disappointment to hunters, for the elk and deer did not come
down where they were easily shot, and but few were killed by
legitimate hunting in the adjoining states. Special attention
was given to the care of these animals by the four scouts employed,
but they were unable to cover the park lines entirely during the
hunting season, and the enlisted men at park stations, to whom
this work was entrusted, were mostly unacquainted with the country, and, in many cases, did not take this duty seriously. I
am satisfied that this part of the protection of the park was
badly neglected, and it was fortunate that the fair weather kept
most of the wild animals up in their summer range in the mountains
beyond the reach of hunters.

From January 5th, nearly every day to March 19th, hay was fed

in the vicinity of Gardiner, and along the road as far as Mammoth Hot Springs, to the deer, mountain sheep, antelope, and about 3,500 elk that came in for it. About 350 tons of hay was fed, of which 100 tons was cut on the field near Gardiner and the balance was purchased from nearby ranches. The wisdom of trying to feed any large number of elk is questionable; but it is necessary to preserve the small numbers of mountain sheep, deer, and particularily the antelope, by supplying them with hay when most needed during the severe winters. The elk, which are much more numerous, can be cared for outside of the park, by saving winter range and raising or buying hay for them in the adjoining forest reserves, but the antelope are too few to risk their loss outside of the park.

Special attention was given to the core of these animals, by our most experienced men, and five additional scouts were hired for this purpose during the winter months, as the troopers who garrisoned the park stations were inexperienced in this line of work. Numbers estimated from 3,000 to 4,000 again left the park and went down the Yellowstone Valley for several miles, apparently not so much in this case by necessity of finding forage, - for the natural food in the park was plentiful and easy to get at all winter, - as much as from force of habit from the preceding winter, when they were starved out by deep snow and severe weather in the park, and found refuge among the haystacks on the ranches below. Again, the U. S. Forest Service and the State Game Wardens cooperated with the

32

National Park Service, to protect these animals against ruthless
slaughter by poachers, with good results. Even then unmistakable
evidence was found in February and March of the killing of fifty
elk by poachers, 34 of which were cows, probably killed for meat,
and 16 bulls, killed for tusks or heads. One or two arrests were
made by the forest rangers, and the accused turned over to the
State Game Warden for trial. Most of these elk returned to the
park in April and May.

ANTELOPE

The antelope wintered in excellent condition, most of them
just inside the north line fence near Gardiner. On November 29th
some dogs from the town of Gardiner got among them and frightened
them badly, and while probably none of them were killed, it was
several weeks before they recovered from their fright and returned
to the alfalfa field and vicinity. A few were killed by coyotes
during the winter, but aside from this the loss was negligible.
About 350 was the largest number seen in any one day, but no
special pains were taken to make a complete count of the herd. The
antelope did not bother about trying to leave the park, as in
previous winters. They became accustomed to the presence of elk on
the feeding grounds, and mingled quite freely with them.

DEER

About the usual number of deer was noted, of both white-
tailed and black-tailed varieties. Slightly more than a hundred
of them, mostly black-tailed, came in for hay during the severe

weather, but most of them remained scattered throughout the mountains along the north line of the park as forage was not hard for them to obtain. Six black-tailed deer were captured by representatives of the U. S. Biological Survey, assisted by our scouts, on April 15th, and shipped to the Montana Bison Range.

ELK

Elk were numerous, tame, and in excellent condition throughout the winter. At least 3,500 of them came down to the feeding grounds around Headquarters and the northern entrance, and those which have acquired the habit of coming down are becoming tamer and more dependent upon the hay each year. While no accurate count was made of the herds of elk during the past year, more than 20,000 were seen in the park in the month of January, with no special effort having been made to count all of them. The Gallatin herd always winters outside of the park, and reports of forest rangers at that time indicated at least 2,000 of the northern herd outside in the forest reserve, north of the park. During the summer many small herds of cows, with their calves, have been seen close to the main roads by tourists and others, and at the present writing it is safe to state that the elk are in first-class condition, with a good crop of calves, and excellent prospects for plenty of food for the coming winter, as the ranges are in

fins shape, due to a very wet summer. The gradual invasion of that
part of the natural winter grazing ground of the elk adjoining the
park, by settlers taking up land, and by grazing permits in the
National Forests, to some extent, threatens the preservation of the
elk, particularly during severe winters, and remedial measures should
be agreed and acted upon, by the States, the Forest Service, and
the National Park Service, at an early date, before it is too late
to do so without great expense. But I seriously question the
theory advanced by some, that they are likely to be entirely exter-
minated by these conditions, as we have sufficient winter range for
fifteen to twenty thousand elk within the boundaries of the park
itself during ordinary winters, and many thousands survived the winter of 1916-17 without leaving or being fed, and this was positively
the hardest winter on record in this country. Representatives of
the United States Forest Service, under direction of the Forester,
Colonel W. T. Graves, have been making a study of this situation
as regards elk grazing in the National Forests near the park, and
are still so engaged. The "Greater Yellowstone" addition to the
park, to include the Teton Mountains on the south, will, if made,
assist in solving the question of winter grazing for the southern
herd of elk, but as this herd winters almost entirely outside of
the park, it would seem that at present the burden or responsibility
rests entirely upon the State of Wyoming and the Forest Service to
reserve for it sufficient winter food. The same may also be said of

the Gallatin herd, which winters in the Gallatin National Forest
in Montana. But these herds belong to the park in summer, and
since their preservation and protection for the benefit of the
public should be and is the aim of all, the full cooperation of the
three parties who can control the situation together, is vital.
This is even more important in handling the northern herd, which
frequently passes back and forth across the park line several
times during the winter. It would seem best, if possible, to provide adequate winter grazing for these elk, rather than to endeavor
to go to the expense of buying or raising hay for common use, as
the latter course is likely to result ultimately in the elk becoming
entirely dependent upon being fed hay in winter. But this is a
problem which is being worked out, and which should be solved and
put into effect soon. Elk from the park herds were shipped and
otherwise disposed of as follows:

Shipped to other states, public parks, etc., under authority
of the National Park Service, at the expense of the parties re-
ceiving them:

To the State of Idaho, February 2, 1918, by freight, in 2
cars..50
To the City of Aurora, Ill., February 18th, by express,
crated.. 2
To the City of Ft. Worth, Texas, February 19th, by express,
crated.. 1
To the City of Crookston, Minn., February 21st, by express,
crated.. 2
To Elk Run, Mont., March 18th, by freight in one car.............25
To the State of Arizona, March 20th, by express in large
car...60

To the City of Mexico, Missouri, March 20th, by express,
crated... 4
To the City of Mexico, Missouri, April 16th, by express, crated,
to replace one shipped earlier, that died on route............ 1
         Total shipped..145
Elk killed by accident in making captures of above for
shipping... 9
Killed by hunters in country adjoining the park during the
open season, and reported.....................................249
Killed by poachers in the National Forest north of the
park.. 50
Killed by poachers inside of the park, and evidence
found... 10
Killed by mountain lions, wolves, and coyotes, and evidence
found... 87
Found dead from unknown causes.................................. 16
         Total known to have been taken from park
herds...568

I regret that in several of the cases of apparent poaching in
the park the evidence was found in the near vicinity of soldier
stations. A black-tailed deer was butchered on the night of October 20th, on the west side of Capitol Hill, in plain sight of my
front door and that of the Commanding Officer, who lived in the adjoining house. Cases of poaching were more frequent than I have
ever known them before, and no arrests were made for this violation
of law.

MOOSE

Moose are frequently seen, and seem to be well scattered over
most of the park. About 50 have been seen in the Upper Yellowstone
country since September 1st. On at least three occasions during
the summer they have been seen from the main road in the park.

BUFFALO

Wild Herd: This herd was located in March on Lamar River and
in Pelican Valley, but not counted. Four calves, present with that
part of the herd seen, indicated a fair increase. They appeared to

have wintered well.

Tame Herd: The tame herd, located on Lamar River, is increasing rapidly and is in excellent condition. There are now a total of 385 animals, namely 176 males and 149 females, from 1 to 22 years old, and 60 calves born during the past summer, sex undetermined. One year ago, October 1, 1917, there were 179 males and 151 females. One 7-year-old bull was disabled and had to be killed on February 29th, and its carcass was donated as a specimen to Hastings College, Nebraska. A 3-year-old cow broke through the ice in the pasture and was drowned on March 8th. A bull calf was hooked to death on April 13th; a 4-year-old bull was found dead on Specimen Ridge in June; and a 4-year-old cow was found dead near the same location on July 1st, in both cases cause unknown. The 1917 crop of calves were vaccinated for hemorrhagic septicemia on November 3rd and again on November 12th, by Dr. F. C. Swaney, a veterinarian of the Department of Agriculture. Under your authority dated November 6th, Dr. Swaney returned on November 16th and 17th, and castrated 60 per cent (44) of the male calves, (20 of the 1916 and 24 of the 1917 crop.) No serious results were noted. The usual show herd of 15 tame buffalo was brought in to Mammoth for the benefit of sightseers at the beginning of the tourist season, but they broke through the fence after about four weeks' stay, and went back to the main herd; and due to shortage of help to herd them we were unable

to bring them back. 270.98 acres of meadow land across the Lamar
River, and about 3 miles above the present buffalo farm, were
plowed during the season of 1917, to be seeded later to grass. Of
this land 65.6 acres were seeded to rye last fall, to be cut this
fall for hay, and has recently been cut and stacked, producing
about 100 tons of good hay. Last spring 65 acres, which was partially disced and harrowed last fall, was cultivated further and
sowed to oats, also with the intention of cutting it for hay, but
the herder quit during the summer and could not be replaced, and
the buffalo tramped this and kept it eaten off until it was too
short to harvest. The balance of the plowed land has been summer
fallowed and more rye will be sowed this fall for next year's hay
crop. Eventually, when this land has been worked sufficiently to
make it smooth, it will be seeded to grass. A half-mile of main
irrigation ditch was built in connection with this cultivated land,
but it is not yet completed. The 200 acres of meadow land was kept
irrigated, and cut for hay. The tame buffalo were grazed most of
the summer on Specimen Ridge, Mount Norris and vicinity.

BEARS

A few grizzly bears were seen during the summer, but they
were not numerous. A large one was caught in a trap in October
to be shipped to the City of Butte, Montana, but broke away and
escaped. Black bears, which were very plentiful, are seen and ad-
mired by everybody, and are one of the greatest attractions in the

park. Naturally shy and inoffensive, the bears in the park are
seen so often and fed by so many people, that they lose all fear,
and as they get older and larger, they often become dangerous and
have to be killed to protect human life and property. In July complaints of the depredations of bears were bitter, and several automobiles were damaged by bears tearing up the upholstery. Nine bears
were killed, and one was found dying near Lake Camp with a bad
would on its head from a stone which laid close by, wielded, probably,
by some angry tourist.

COYOTES AND WOLVES

These animals have done much damage to other game, and for
that reason much pains have been taken to hunt them down and trap
them. Two expert hunters were employed as scouts during the winter,
and spent most of their time hunting and trapping. Steve Elkins,
the famous guide and mountain lion hunter, was also employed for
several weeks with his pack of lion hounds hunting lions, wolves,
and coyotes, and the U.S. Biological Survey sent one of its hunters
here for a time last spring, but he was not so successful as were
some of our own men, and was finally called away by the draft. A-
nother Biological Survey hunter, Mr. Wm. D. Clemons, has been work-
ing on the Upper Yellowstone since August 1st, and is trapping and
hunting wolves and coyotes along the park line, on both sides of it.
In all 190 coyotes and 36 wolves were killed in the park during the
year. While there are more of thes animals in the park than are

desirable, I am of the opinion that there are not so many found among the game animals as there are among domestic animals in farming communities outside, as I have been informed by the State Game Warden of Montana that during 1917 there were killed 848 coyotes in the County of Galletin, 1533 in Park and Sweetgrass Counties, and 301 in Carbon County.

MOUNTAIN LIONS

Twenty-three mountain lions were killed in the park during the year. These were hunted by Steve Elkins and Scout Anderson, with trained dogs.

MOUNTAIN SHEEP

Mountain sheep seemed to be thriving and were seen frequently during the winter along the road to Gardiner. The winter was so mild that the sheep seldom came down for hay, and our attempt to bait them into a corral, to capture and dip them for sheep scab, failed. But no sign of the scab, which was in evidence the previous winter, was noticed on them, and it was hardly necessary to treat them. The Mount Evert's band can usually be found within an hour's ride from Headquarters, from October to May, inclusive, and are easy to approach and photograph. Fourteen fine rams were seen and approached by parties on saddle horses to within a hundred feet on the north end of Mount Everts on May 7th.

BEAVER

These most interesting animals are in evidence in nearly every

stream in the park. Their dams and houses may be seen from several points along the main roads, and they can be seen at work if one cares to take the pains to visit their homes just before dark.

OTHER ANIMALS

Porcupines, which a few years ago seemed to have disappeared from the park, are now numerous and are frequently seen along the roads. Rabbits, gophers, red squirrels, chipmunks, and woodchucks, are much in evidence, and are seen by all visitors. Lynx, bobcats, foxes, otter, martin, mink, weasels, conies, skunks, muskrats, etc., are found, but are not often seen.

The development and protection of the wild animal life in the park, which was only considered of secondary interest for many years, has become to be generally known as a feature of utmost importance to the public. Our animals are becoming tamer and more is seen of them, from year to year; and I doubt if anything in the park creates a more lasting interest and pleasure in the minds of most tourists than does a small herd of elk or a few scattering deer seen along the road; a herd of bison in the pasture at Mammoth, or on Lamar River, where the main herd is kept; a porcupine along the roadside, which the driver will be careful to avoid, if his car is not equipped with puncture-proof tires, and best of all, the bears, which frequent the camps and hotels, where they beg for food, although they are already so fat that they can

hardly climb a tree if startled. And in winter it is well worth
a trip across the continent to see the herds of elk, deer, anto-
lope, and mountain sheep that may be found at or near the northern entrance. It is certainly a paradise for moving picture
artists, in search of pictures from real life, that will always
command interest before any audience.

DISEASE OF ANIMALS

Arrangements were made to capture and dip for scab, the
small band of mountain sheep that winters on Mount Everts and
in Gardiner Canyon, but the winter was so mild that they did not
often come down for hay, and as there was no evidence of the scab
appearing again, the work was postponed.

The tame buffalo calves were, as usual, vaccinated last fall
against hemorrhagic septicemia.

A few buffalo cows from the tame herd, which were known or
suspected of habitual abortion, were seperated from the main
herd for the period when the disease is most likely to be contagious, and sample of stomach contents of an aborted calf were
forwarded to the Bureau of Animal Industry, Washington, D. C.,
for examination and analysis. If this disease is the contagious
form, it is not especially prevalent.

BIRDS

Nearly two hundred varieties of birds have been noted in the
park as summer residents, and are listed in our Circular of Information, which is distributed to visitors. Quite a number of

these remain during the winter. Canada Geese, ducks, and other
waterfowl on the lakes and rivers are very tame, and of much
interest to tourists.

PROTECTION OF GAME

The Sundry Civil Bill, approved June 12, 1917, (Public
No. 21, 65th Congress) which provides funds for National Parks,
provided that "No part of this appropriation or the revenues of
the Yellowstone National Park shall be used for payment of salaries for the protection of the park, authorized by the act of
March third, eighteen hundred and eighty-three, to be performed
by the detail of troops." This legislation made it necessary to
re-garrison Fort Yellowstone which, by mutual consent of the War
and Interior Departments, had been abandoned on October 1, 1916,
and a squadron of Cavalry arrived on June 26, 1917, and such
duties as pertained to protection of the game, &c., in the park,
devolved upon the commanding officer. These troops were inexperienced in work such as pertains to protection of national parks
and wild animals, and were not properly equipped so far as transportation and other necessary articles are concerned. On December
22d this squadron was relieved by one troop of Cavalry from
another regiment, even less experienced in the class of work which
they were sent for. Arriving so late in the season, they had no
opportunity whatever to acquaint themselves with the territory to
be covered in protecting the game animals, and were able to do but

little good in this direction during the winter. These conditions
were not conducive to successful work in the line of protecting
the wild animals in the park, and the results are shown by the
lack of arrests for poaching and other violations of law, and the
evidences of poaching and violations which have been noted.

VIOLATIONS OF LAW

At least nine cases of violation of the law regarding the
killing of wild animals were recorded, but no arrests were made,
and the evidence was not sufficient to take action in any case.
One of these, the killing of a black-tailed deer, occurred on the
grounds near Fort Yellowstone, and two elk were killed within a
few hundred yards of the Gallatin Soldier Station, which burned
soon afterwards, and which was garrisoned by a sergeant and one
man, who are both under charges at the present time for stealing
automobile tires in the park and trying to sell them in Gardiner,
the latter part of August.

Camp fires have been left burning in a few instances, but
usually at one of the regular main camping places, where they
were soon discovered and extinguished without any damage having
occured.

The regulation prohibiting the sale or serving of intoxicating
liquor in the park, and the Federal Law, prohibiting its being
introduced into military camps or quarters, have together acted as
a deterrent in keeping it out of the park during the past year.
But considerable difficulty has been had by the military authorities

by worthless characters in the town of Gardiner furnishing it to
enlisted men, indirectly, and the Commanding Officer has usually
found it necessary to maintain a military guard at the soldier
station near the town. Two men, whom the Commanding Officer was
satisfied were furnishing whiskey to his men, were, at his request,
debarred from entering the park on the ground that they were un-
desirable, and the order debarring them is still in force.

On July 25th a tourist stopping at Upper Geyser Basin was ar-
rested on the charge of treasonable utterances, and his case has been
turned over to the Department of Justice at his home in Memphis,
Tenn., for proper action.

On September 23d complaint was filed with the United States
Commissioner against John McPherson, of Gardiner, Mont., for trans-
porting tourists through the park without proper license. He
was tried September 26th, pled guilty, and was fined $50.00 and
costs.

SANITATION AND HEALTH PRECAUTIONS

The special camps for automobile tourists were maintained
at Mammoth, Upper Basin, Lake, and Canyon, and were appreciated.
They were kept supplied with fuel for camp fires, and cleaned up
as often as men could be spared to do the work.

On the basis of a complaint to the National Park Service late
in the summer of 1917, to the effect that the water used by the
Hotel Company at Upper Geyser Basin was not good, the United States

46

Public Health Service cent its laboratory car "Hamilton" to
Gardinor, arriving on June 8th, in charge of Lieutenant Everett
Judson and his corps of four assistants. Automobile and truck
transportation, and such assistance as practicable, were furnished
him, and during the following four weeks he made a careful test
of all waters in the park that are ever used for drinking or
culinary purposes. While his report has not be received, he made
a few suggestions of immediate necessity in regard to the water in use
at some points, more particularly at the Upper Basin Camp, which
was presumed to be particularly good, but which he found dangerous.
The Camping Company took immediate action, and boiled all drinking
water until they could make a connection with the reservoir of the
Hotel Company, where the water was found to be especially good.

All milk cows in use in the park for furnishing fresh milk to
the public were given the tuberculin test by inspectors of the
Bureau of Animal Industry, before the opening of the tourist season.

There is much to be done in the park in the way of improvement
in sanitation, especially around the permanent camps.

FIRE

No forest fires of any consequence occurred during the year.
The past season was so unusually wet that there were but few days
when there was any danger of a fire spreading to any great extent,
had any started.

47

The Gallatin Soldier Station, located about one mile inside
of the park on the County road leading into the park from the northwest corner, was destroyed by fire on the afternoon of Sunday,
March 10th, while occupied by a non-commissioned officer and a
private belonging to Troop "C" 11th Cavalry. This station was
built by the War Department in 1910, at a cost of $5,518.00. The
men at the station claimed that the fire started from a defective
concrete chimney which showed cracks large enough to emit sparks.
A new log ranger station, to take the place of this one, has been
built on the park line, about a mile from the site of the old one,
and a small log barn has been built in connection with it. The old
barn was not destroyed, but it is too cumbersome to permit its being
moved to the new site.

IMPROVEMENTS

Telephone lines: During the season of 1917 a total of 40-1/2
miles of telephone line was rebuilt at an average cost of $162.33
per mile, and 143 miles were repaired - mostly heavy repairs - at
an average cost of about $90 per mile, the most of which was in-
cluded in my last annual report. Eight miles of new line were constructed late last fall, between Mammoth and Soda Butte Station, and
the balance of this line was repaired so it would do until it could
be rebuilt. There are still 27 miles of this line in a bad state
of repair, which should be rebuilt as soon as labor can be procured
to do the work. The material is all on hand, and poles were cut

during the past summer, peeled and skidded so as to dry out and
season well before they are used. A new switchboard was purchased
to replace the old one at Headquarters, and this is now being installed. No heavy repairs, or construction work, has been undertaken during the present season, due to lack of labor.

Firelanes: The extensive work of constructing and rebuilding
firelanes, was continued to early in November, when it became necessary to stop on account of bad weather. The total work of firelanes
during the last fiscal year, most of which is listed in my annual
report for 1917, consisted, up to December 31, 1917, in constructing
111-1/2 miles at an average cost per mile of $47.32, rebuilding 79
miles at an average cost of $43.08 per mile, and repairing 175-1/2
miles at an average cost of $14.89 per mile. During May and June of
this year a new firelane was constructed from a point on Yellowstone
River about 3 miles above Gardiner, along the north bank of the
river to Slough Creek, a total distance of about 20 miles, at a
cost of $96.60 per mile. While this was rather expensive, due to
the fact that about 2 miles of it was through granite boulders and
slide rock, it will be most useful as a trail, as it can be used by
pack animals throughout the winter, being located where but little
snow falls, and makes the winter habitats of wild game easy of suc-
cess.

Two men with saddle and pack animals have been employed during
August and September in going over the trails and cutting out the

fallen timber and making other slight necessary repairs. 275 miles
were covered.

Marking boundary lines: About 21-1/2 miles of the north line of
the park between Gardiner and Slough Creek were cut out on the line
and blazed through the timber and marked by placing additional
monuments close enough together so they could be seen through the
open places. This work is important, as in many places this line
was not plainly enough marked for hunters who were not acquainted
with the country, and they frequently got in trouble by getting into the park with unsealed firearms.

SIGNS

A complete list of metal signs for roads, trails, objects of
interest, needed for the guidance of the public, was made up,
and the signs will soon be delivered.

Buildings: During June a new ranger station was built at the
northwest corner of the park, to replace the Gallatin Soldier
Station which was burned in March. The new building consists of a
one-story log house 16 x 50 feet, with log annex for kitchen
16 x 16 feet, and a porte cochere in front, large enough to permit an automobile to drive in while being registered. All with
shingled roof, ceiled inside throughout, and the main building
divided by two partitions into three rooms. Double floor, brick
chimney, walls chinked inside and plastered outside. The material
for floors, trimmings, etc., was hauled in over very bad spring

roads, under great difficulties. The logs were cut near by in the park. A substantial log barn 16 x 16 feet in size, with dirt roof, was also constructed in connection with the house.

Cultivation of land: One hundred and seventy-nine acres of land was plowed on Lamar River, about 3 miles above the present buffalo farm and on the opposite side, in addition to about a hundred acres plowed last season and reported fall of 1917. This makes a total of 270.9 acres of land now under cultivation there preparatory to seeding it to grass for hay for tame buffalo and other animals, which is now in various stages of cultivation, as noted herein under the heading of "Buffalo". Half a mile of main / ditch was also constructed in connection with the cultivation of this land. The alfalfa field at northern entrance, containing 45-1/2 acres, became foul from weeds and foxtail and was plowed up and sowed to oats to be cut as a forage crop.

About two hundred tons of wild hay has been cut at Yancey and Norris, for subsistence of work teams and saddle and pack animals. Some of this will be baled and some fed from the stack. At present price of hay, this will effect a large saving, and more would have been harvested but for scarcity of labor.

NATURAL PHENOMENA

The small geyser that broke out at Norris in the timber across the road from the Black Growler last season, showed no activity during the summer.

51

A pool near the road at the 15-mile post south from Mammoth Hot Springs, played muddy water to a height of about 40 feet, several times during the summer.

At Mammoth Hot Springs, the overflow from the large spring partially changed its course back to the south side, but the greater part of its overflow is still over the north side of the terrace. Hymen Terrace was active most of the summer, but has recently died out again, which is a common occurence with this terrace.

ACCIDENTS

No serious accidents to regular transportation care were recorded, and in but few cases to private automobiles.

On June 10th, an employee of the Transportation Company ran his private automobile - a new "Dodge" car - over the precipice into the canyon of the Yellowstone River at the Needles, about 1/4 mile below the mouth of Tower Creek. He scrambled out as the car was going over the edge. The bank at this point is several hundred feet in height and practically perpendicular. The Yellowstone River was at its highest stage, and the car evidently struck the water, for no trace of it could be found until several weeks later fragments large enough to be recognized as belonging to a "Dodge" car were found about a half a mile below.

On two occasions "Ford" cars belonging to the Yellowstone Park Camping Company, and in use for that company, have been overturned or run over the bank. On both occasions the driver came

out without injury, but his companion was injured, - once having
an ankle broken, and the other instance the pelvic bone was injured.

On September 6th a "Cadillac" car was overturned at Cub
Creek, on the Cody entrance road, injuring one lady in the party
quite seriously. Luckily two other cars arrived on the scene
within two or three minutes afterwards, and took the occupants in
to the Lake Outlet, where they were cared for by the keeper. The
Army Surgeon from Fort Yellowstone went out with the Hotel Company's
ambulance, and gave them medical attention, and next day they returned home by rail from Yellowstone, Montana.

On July 21st Sergeant Arthur S. Brewer and Private Victor
Manterfield, both of Troop "G", 11th Cavalry, stationed in the
park, were fishing from a small boat in a lake near Soda Butte
Station, and the boat overturned and both were drowned. The
exact details of the accident are not known, as no one else was
present at the time.

On August 30th, Mr. Frank P. Prichard, of Philadelphia, who
was touring the park with the regular companies, died suddenly
from heart trouble in the dining room at Canyon Camp.

PERSONNEL

The title of "Supervisor" of various National Parks, was
changed to "Superintendent", effective November 1, 1917.

Due to the great demand for labor everywhere, on account of
the World War, it has been necessary to curtail much work that,

under other conditions, should be done, and to devote such
energies as were available to necessary maintenance, and re-
placements caused by floods, fire, etc. Naturally, it costs
much more to accomplish results than when times are normal,
and this is not entirely due to high cost of labor and supplies,
but partially to the fact that efficiency cannot be secured
when men do not care whether they work or not, for they know
they can go elsewhere and get employment at a high rate of pay when-
ever they feel like it.

Many excellent permanent employees have been lost because
they were drafted, or desired to secure positions closer to the
War. The operations of the draft, including registry of men on
dates fixed; subscriptions to Liberty Loans and War Savings; Red
Cross work, etc., all have taken much time from other duties. But
these additional duties have been faithfully and cheerfully performed, with a keen realization of the fact that our first duty
lies in doing what we can in that direction. Subscriptions to the
Second and Third Liberty Loans from employees amounted to $9,700.00,
and War Savings Stamps to the amount of $1,700.90 were purchased.
In December last a Branch of the Red Cross was organized among park
employees with a membership of about 120, which has since been in-
creased to about 130. Funds have been collected and turned in to
the Chapter amounting in all to $1,932.58, and much work in the
line of knitting, sewing, etc., has been accomplished by the ladies
of the branch.

54

RECOMMENDATIONS

The addition to the Yellowstone Park of a large tract of land south of and adjoining the park, to include Jackson Lake and the Teton Mountains, would be an everlasting public benefit. This proposed addition includes mountain scenery, which is comparable to the finest in the world.

Honorable Franklin K. Lane, The Secretary of the Interior, visited the park October 7th to 8th, 1917, making the trip from Yellowstone to Upper Basin, Thumb, side trip to Moran, Wyoming; Lake, Canyon, Tower Falls, Mammoth, side trip to Gardiner; Norris, and back to Yellowstone. Several suggestions made by him relative to signs, guard-rails, and clearing of timber along the roads, so as to afford a better view of the road ahead, and of interesting features, have been complied with as far as practicable.

Mr. Horace M. Albright, Assistant Director of National Parks, was in the park and vicinity June 27th to August 15th, 1918, assisting in the organization of a ranger force to take the place of troops, the taking over of the improvement and maintenance of work from the War Department.

Very respectfully,

CHESTER A. LINDSLEY

Acting Superintendent.

CPSIA information can be obtained
at www.ICGtesting.com
Printed in the USA
BVHW040811280119
538836BV00014B/302/P